First Facts®

Earn It, Save It, Spend It!

Save Money

by Mary Reina

raintree

a Capstone company — publishers for children

Raintree is an imprint of Capstone Global Library Limited, a company incorporated in England and Wales having its registered office at 264 Banbury Road, Oxford, OX2 7DY – Registered company number: 6695582

www.raintree.co.uk
myorders@raintree.co.uk

Edited by Karen Aleo
Designed by Sarah Bennett
Picture research by Tracy Cummins
Production by Kathy McColley
Originated by Capstone Global Library Ltd
Printed and bound in India

ISBN 978 1 4747 8157 2 (hardback)
ISBN 978 1 4747 8161 9 (paperback)

British Library Cataloguing in Publication Data
A full catalogue record for this book is available from the British Library.

Acknowledgements
Alamy: Tetra Images, LLC, 19; Capstone Studio: Karon Dubke, Design Element, 17; iStockphoto: Alina555, 13, ivanastar, 7 Right, SelectStock, 11; Shutterstock: Adam Gilchrist, Back Cover, anythings, 21, Doubletree Studio, 15, Forgem, Design Element, Monkey Business Images, 5, monticello, 7 Left, Nik Merkulov, Design Element, olavs, Cover, Sergey Ryzhov, 9

Every effort has been made to contact copyright holders of material reproduced in this book. Any omissions will be rectified in subsequent printings if notice is given to the publisher.

All the internet addresses (URLs) given in this book were valid at the time of going to press. However, due to the dynamic nature of the internet, some addresses may have changed, or sites may have changed or ceased to exist since publication. While the author and publisher regret any inconvenience this may cause readers, no responsibility for any such changes can be accepted by either the author or the publisher. Every effort has been made to contact copyright holders of material reproduced in this book. Any omissions will be rectified in subsequent printings if notice is given to the publisher.

Contents

CHAPTER 1

It's great to save

Everybody needs money. One of the best ways to have money is to **save** it. Instead of spending your money all at once, you put it aside and add more when you can. Saving money means you can buy the things you need and the things you want.

Fact

Saving money can help you afford more expensive things. You may not get enough money each week to buy something you really want. But if you save a little each week, you will be able to buy it later.

save to put money away so you have it in the future

What is the difference between a need and a want? Needs are things you must have. Food, clothes and school supplies are needs. You might like wants, but can do without them. Video games, toys and tickets to the cinema are wants.

Needs

Wants

7

You may not save enough money
to buy all your needs and wants.
Then you will have to make a choice.
Your needs should come first. You
can still buy some of your wants.
All you have to do is keep saving.

Needs and wants

How do you choose between needs
and wants? Let's look at an example.
You need pens for school. You want the
glitter pens because a friend has them.
Needs are more important than wants.
You might buy a cheaper set of pens to
save money.

CHAPTER 2

Saving choices

It's easy to save at home with a glass jar. Fill the jar with money you **earn**. Some young people earn money by helping at home. Others get **pocket money**. Some get money as a gift for birthdays and holidays. If you don't spend it straight away, you can add the money you get to the jar.

earn to receive payment for working

pocket money money given to someone regularly, usually each week

A **savings account** at a bank is another way to save. An adult can help you open an account. Banks are places that hold money and keep it safe. You fill out a slip to **deposit** money in the account. You fill out another slip to **withdraw** money. You can check your account online too.

> ### FACT
> Banks offer different types of accounts. Some are good for saving money for a long time. Others are better if you think you will need to take your money out again soon.

savings account an account at the bank in which you store money

deposit to put money into a bank account

withdraw to take money out of a bank account

A good thing about saving your money in a bank is that the bank will give you **interest**. Interest is the small amount of money that the bank adds to your savings. Over time, this will help your savings to grow.

FACT

Interest can also work in a less positive way. Banks lend money to people who need it. This is called a **loan**. Banks charge interest for the loan. So the person who has borrowed the money has to pay back the amount of the loan, plus the interest on top.

interest money added to your savings by a bank. Also, the cost of borrowing money

loan money that is borrowed with a plan to pay it back

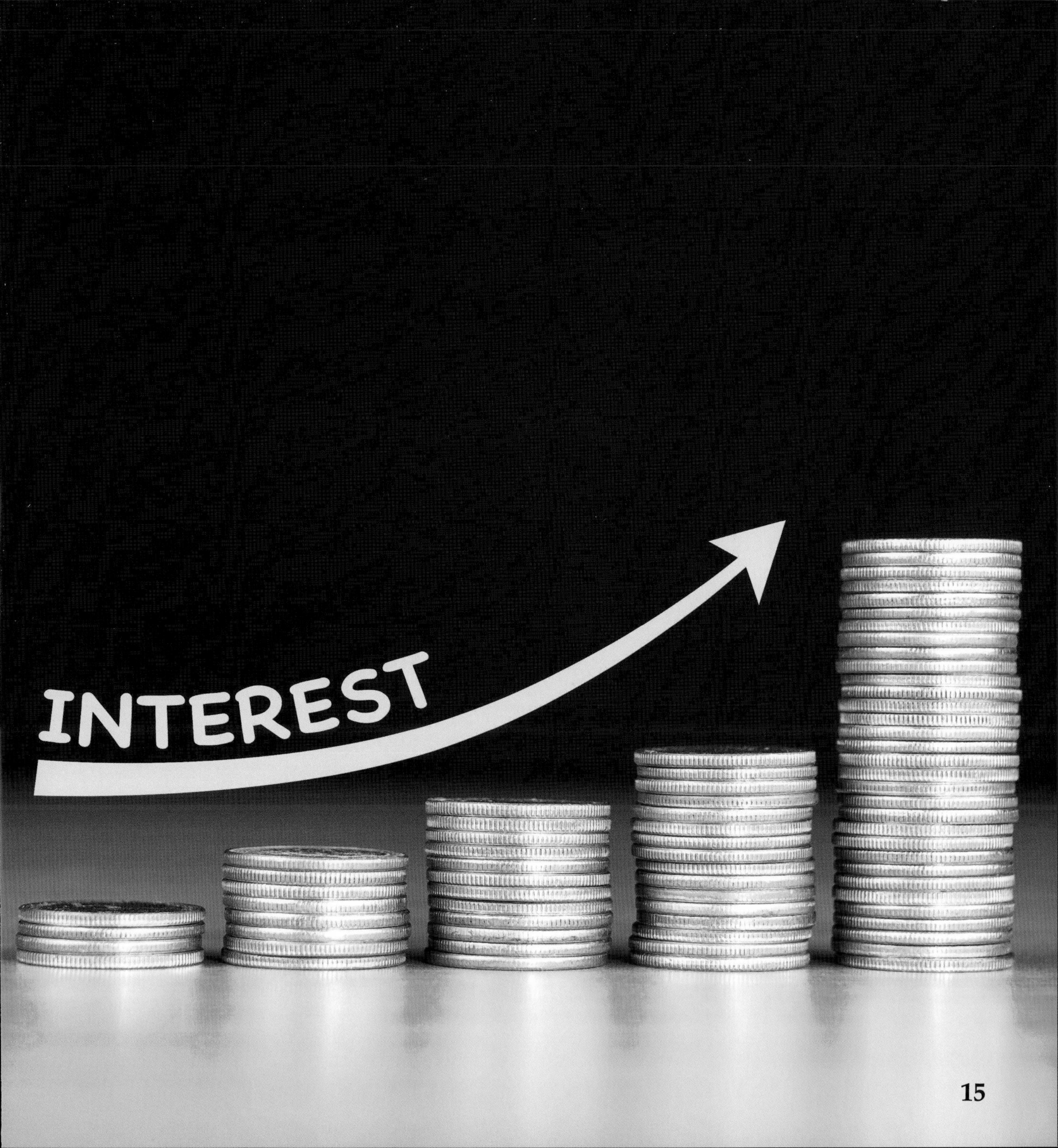
INTEREST

CHAPTER 3

Try it!

Here is a fun way to help you keep track of your savings. An adult can help you set up this project. It will show how money goes into and comes out of a savings account. It will also help you save for the future. All you need is a jar and a notebook.

Set up a page in the notebook like the savings chart opposite. Fill in the chart each time you save money. Do the same when you take money out to spend. Count the money that is left. Write the amount on the chart.

Keep saving

When the jar fills up, you can put the money in a savings account. Then start filling the jar again. You can add it to the savings account, buy something special or **donate** it. When you donate money, you give it to a person in need.

donate to give something as a gift to a charity or cause

Savings chart

Date	Deposit	Withdraw	Total money saved
1 December	£1.00		£1.00
15 December		£0.50	£0.50
10 January	£2.00		£2.50

Try to fill the jar by a certain date. You could pick your next birthday. You might pick a favourite school holiday. Saving enough to fill the jar will depend on the choices you make.

You will always have needs and wants. Saving money will make it easier to buy them.

Glossary

deposit to put money into a bank account

donate to give something as a gift to a charity or cause

earn to receive payment for working

interest money added to your savings by a bank. Also, the cost of borrowing money

loan money that is borrowed with a plan to pay it back

pocket money money given to someone regularly, usually each week

save to put money away so you have it in the future

savings account an account at the bank in which you store money

withdraw to take money out of a bank account

Find out more

Managing Your Money, Jane Bingham and Holly Bathie (Usborne, 2019)

The Kids' Money Book: Earning, Saving Spending, Investing, Donating (Jamie Kyle McGillian (Sterling, 2016)

Wants Versus Needs series, Linda Staniford (Raintree, 2015)

Websites and apps

Try the Rooster Money app. It helps you keep track of your pocket money and your spending. You can also set goals for saving.

These websites have fun games and videos to help you understand money and make good spending choices:

www.bbc.com/bitesize/topics/zp8dmp3
www.bbc.com/bitesize/topics/z8yv4wx

Comprehension questions

1. Pretend you are thinking about buying a new backpack for school. The one you have is still good. Is it a need or a want?

2. How can you invest money?

3. What are reasons for saving?

Index